Backyard Books

Are you a Snail?

KINGFISHER

a Houghton Mifflin Company imprint
222 Berkeley Street
Boston, Massachusetts 02116
www.houghtonmifflinbooks.com

First published in hardcover in 2000
First published in paperback in 2003

2 4 6 8 10 9 7 5 3 1

(PB) 1TR/1202/TWP/DIG(MA)/170SEM

LIBRARY OF CONGRESS CATALOGING-IN-PUBLICATION DATA
Allen, Judy.
Are you a snail?/by Judy Allen; illustrated by Tudor Humphries.—1st ed.
p. cm.— (Backyard Books)
Summary: Introduces the life cycle of a snail, showing how it changes from an egg to
an adult snail.
1. Snails—Juvenile literature. [1. Snails.] I. Title. II. Series. III. Humphries, Tudor, ill.

QL430.4 . A59 2000
594'.3 21—dc21
99-042382

Editor: Katie Puckett
Coordinating Editor: Laura Marshall
Series Designer: Jane Tassie

Printed in Singapore

ISBN 0-7534-5242-1 (HC)
ISBN 0-7534-5604-4 (PB)

Backyard Books

Are you a Snail?

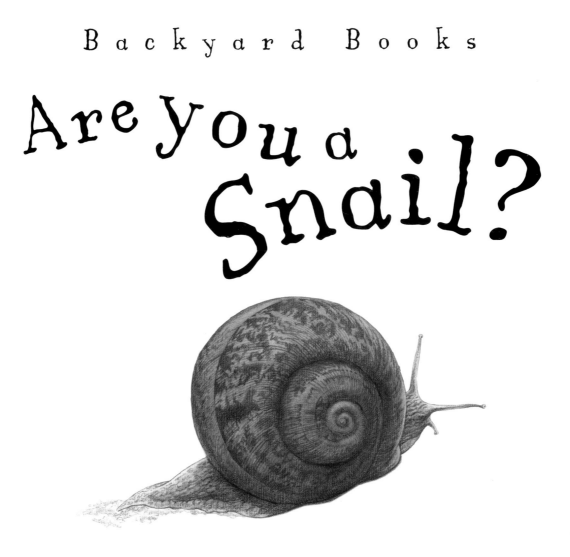

Judy Allen and Tudor Humphries

KINGFISHER

Are you a snail?

If you are, your life began in
an egg like one of these.

When you hatch, you look like this.
This is your mother.

You are much smaller
than your mother.

You are very, very small,

but you will grOW.

You have two horns and two
eyes on stalks.

You can pull your eyes right down
inside the stalks and into your
head if you need to.

You are slimy. You are VERY slimy.

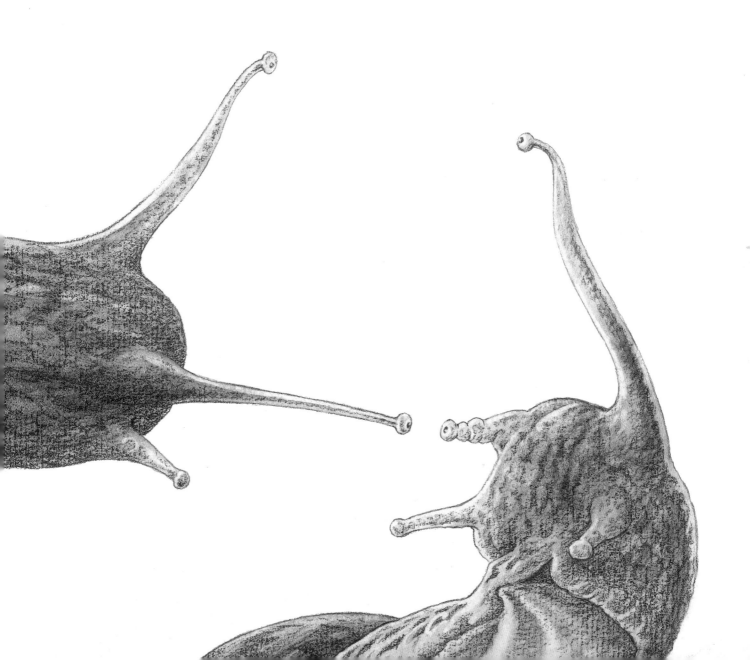

You have a shell
with a beautiful
pattern on it.

You have no
legs and only
one foot, but it
is a strong foot.

The slime on your strong
foot helps you
slide along.

Wherever you go,
you leave a silvery, slimy trail.

You like damp places.

You like to be outside
when it has rained.

You have a big, rough tongue
right inside of your mouth.
Use it to rip pieces
off of leaves and
eat them.

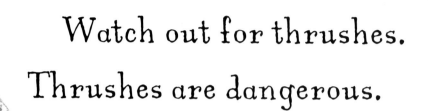

Watch out for thrushes.
Thrushes are dangerous.

They like to eat snails.

They know how to break the shells off,
and they don't mind the slime.

Hide in the daytime. Go out at night
when the thrushes are asleep.

Look out for foxes.

Foxes are dangerous.

Hungry foxes eat snails, and they don't mind the slime either.

Foxes go out at night, but you can't hide at night because you need to eat sometime. Just be careful.

Do not go where humans go.
You could get squashed. You move
too slowly to get out of the way.

Humans don't like you because you
eat their plants. They might put poison
or sharp gravel in the garden.

It hurts to walk on gravel.
Also, it sticks to your slime.

And poison? Poison is poisonous!

You may meet someone who looks like this.

It is not a snail whose shell has fallen off. This is a slug.

The winter cold makes
you sleepy. Find a safe place.

Your slime hardens into
a door in your shell.

The spring warmth
wakes you. Dribble on the
inside of your shell door. It melts away.

Slime off and find food.

However, if you look a little

or this

like this   or this

or this

you are

not a snail.

You are . . .

. . . a human child.

You have no shell on your back.
You have no horns and your
eyes are not on stalks.

But you can do a lot of things that
snails can't do.

You are not afraid
of thrushes or foxes.

Most humans like you.

Best of all, you are not
in the least bit
slimy.

Did You Know . . .

. . . the trail of a
snail is broken, but the
trail of a slug is one long line of slime.

. . . there are more than 60,000
different kinds of snails.

. . . this is a garden snail,
but there are other kinds that live
in deserts or swamps, in ponds or
rivers, or in the sea.

. . . the Giant
African snail
can grow very large.
The biggest one ever found was almost
16 inches long and weighed two pounds!

. . . snails belong to a family of creatures
called gastropods, which
means "stomach-foot."
So you could say a snail is a
stomach on
a foot.